Cranberry Beads

Karin Stangl

❧

Cranberry Beads

Cranberry Beads

Copyright ©2016 Karin Stangl

ISBN: 978-1-940769-53-0

Publisher: Mercury HeartLink

Printed in the United States of America

Permission is granted to educators to create copies of individual poems for classroom or workshop assignments.

Contact Karin Stangl, editor:

mariposa_verde@q.com

Poems

Cranberry Beads

for my
Grandmother
Ruth E. Cooper

CRANBERRY BEADS

Life's work.
Aspirations,
Memories,
Reflections,
Regrets,
Suffering,
Sarcasm,
Survival stories,
Career choices,
Fleeting joys,
Tensile encounters,
Expressions uninhibited,
Challenges met –
And pierced through
With an ambitious,
Sometimes headstrong needle.
A threaded oral history
Of experiences
I wear now…
Strung together
Like cranberry beads,
Fastened with a silver clasp.

Rain Stick

The drought is mocked
By an inverted stick
That triggers the rapid passage
Of small seeds
From end to end…
Flowing,
Rippling,
Mimicking
Pregnant drops
Of quenching rain
On a blue, tin roof.

CAROUSEL

Calliope tunes
Promise delight,
Fulfillment,
And the coveted brass ring.
Blue tufts of cotton candy,
Held precariously in one hand,
Dissolve on the tongue
Ever....so sweetly.
Whimsical colors of high-gloss paint
Churn, rise, and fall to the melody.
In a tranquilizing blur of color and light,
Wooden horses revolve,
But never reach
Their destination.

AGE IS A MATTER OF MIND

Although the mirror's reflections,
Show more imperfections,
In need of correction,
The older I get...

I have more affection
For my body's collection
Of mismatched...sections
The older I get...

In retrospection,
I have a better complexion.
I can handle rejection,
And others' detection
Of flaws in me,
The older I get...

I mean...after all this dissection,
And acute introspection,
Who is really perfection,
Without a few injections,
Or facial corrections,
The older we get?

High Jumper

Urban street below
Is grey, dizzying, steep
The mounted steed hesitates.
Urged on, it straddles the precipice.
Midair, aloft,
The rider dares not look down.
She steels her eyes ahead
Focused on the goal.
Moves ahead.
Moves onward.
The familiar hollow galloping sound
Of hoofs making contact
With grass signals
Another challenge met,
And overcome.
The jump perfected.
Surmounting yet another
Glass ceiling.

THE PRETENDER
(High School Class Reunion - 1995)

Her golden earrings dance.
She shifts her beaded clutch purse
From arm to arm.
Drink in hand,
She struts.
She glistens.
Stiletto heels cut through
The crowded room.

Confronting me is her face.
Beaming,
Curious,
Annoying.

"Remember me?,"
She chatters, as she
Forces me into a hug.
No name is offered.

Neurons race
To make a connection,
Probing every corner
Of my mind
For a name.

No recall.
"We must have had
A class together," I say.
That's sufficiently vague,
Smiling a little "white lie" smile,
To mask the emptiness.

"Don't you remember?,"
She says, with a lofty tone,
"I sat behind you in the 7th grade."
"We were neighbors."
"We were in Girl Scouts together."

My mind and I
Have a private discussion.
"I lived in Wyoming in the 7th grade."
"She was never my neighbor."
"I was never a Girl Scout."
She is deluded.

This charade must end.
But, it is not polite
To be abrupt.

"Nice to see you again," she says.
"We sure had some good times,
"Didn't we?," she chirps.
"Nice to see <u>you</u> again, too," I parrot.

I watch her departure.
Her golden earrings dance.
She shifts her beaded clutch purse
From arm to arm.
Drink in hand,
She struts.
She glistens.
Stiletto heels cut through
The crowded room.

She walks alone in the
Shallow illusion
Of popularity.

Paradox

Which do I choose?

A sage green mat
Trimmed with flamboyant violet edging
And a black, lacquer frame that
Focuses the petunias strikingly in the center?

Enhance the contrasts?

Or, a mat of subdued earth tones
Trimmed in a subtle-edge color that
Plays off the leaves instead,
With a traditional gold frame?

Enhance the similarities?

How does one frame
The poetry of things?

PANDEMONIUM

Blood, adrenaline, and pandemonium
Fuse with floating grey particles
Of drywall, ash, concrete, and debris
Raining on the streets.
A nation watches
In speechless desperation.
The unthinkable is reality.
Who can forget…
The man and woman holding hands,
Who plunge from a 100th story window.
Glass shatters.
Fire consumes.
Steel buckles.
Icons topple.
In a crucible of fear and anguish,
Strength of spirit prevails.
Americans weep
And discover the resolve
To send their children
To war.

September 11, 2001

Morning Song and Sand
White Sands, New Mexico

Lark song penetrates
The ominous silence.
The smell of rosemary mint
Is carried on the breeze.
Glistening grains of windswept white
Meander into mounds.
A vast, arid vista
Appears lifeless,
Except for shadowed footprints
Of the nocturnal ones –
An Apache pocket mouse,
A darkling beetle,
A bleached, earless lizard.
Sand verbena stands in pink defiance
Against a rippling sea of white.

ODE TO FRUITCAKE

Odious loaf.
Of this gift – be wary.
Full of rancid nuts,
And candied cherries.

Molasses brown.
Three inches thick.
Egg-laden and heavy,
Like a brick.

Leaves syrup residue,
Upon one's fingers.
From year to year,
The gift that lingers.

Only saving grace,
With rum it's laced.
But even liquor can't
Improve the taste.

Shrouded in plastic
On a top pantry shelf,
It can sit for years
All by itself.

Fruitcakes yearly face
The same dismal fate.
Each destined to become
A paperweight.

Why preserve the "Christmas Curse"?
Why not defeat it?
Even the world's starving children
Would refuse to eat it.

Vanquish the guilt
When it first comes in –
Just pitch the cake,
And save the tin.

Sunset on the Willow Flowage

Willow Flowage is encapsulated
By lush, green foliage.
Isolated and serene.

A buffer of aspen
And scattered pines
Stipple the shoreline.

Silhouetted eagles and osprey
Soar home for the night,
To nest in tall branches.

The sunset blushes
In tangerine and pomegranate hues.

Splashes of vibrant color
Are mirrored in water
That laps rhythmically
At the shore's edge.

Loon song pierces the silence
Shrill and soulful.

Then...all is still.

Darkness gives way.
To the wake
Of a full,
Butter-yellow moon.

Thank You to A. A. Milne

Kanga, Piglet, Eeyore,
Tigger and Roo,
What are more whimsy
Than friends of the Pooh?

Delightful the trip
To Buckingham Palace
When Christopher Robin
Went down with Alice.

The quest for honey
And Eeyore's tail
Meeting the heffalump
In such sprightly detail.

Reliving the joy in small eyes
As each page makes its debut,
What are more whimsy
Than friends of the Pooh?

SAVOR THE WINE AND CHOCOLATE

Damp chill outside,
Warmed by the prospect
Of fine, garnet-colored wines inside.
Downpour of droplets on the tent
Are repelled.
Fetzer winery attracts
Throngs of tasters
For a delectable,
Wine and chocolate-savoring experience.
Temptation lilts over the tongue
And teases:

Raspberry chocolate truffles and red zinfandel
      – one ticket.
Chocolate mousse and some reserve cabernet
      – one ticket.
Chocolate-dipped strawberries and a pinot noir
      – one ticket.
Chocolate cheesecake and a fine merlot
      – one ticket.

Cleanse the palate with
More dark, bittersweet, butter smoothness.
Then, swirl, smell, swish, swill, and swallow
Some ruby-red ecstasy.

Tickets gone, we depart.
With a flushed smile,
A Valentine's Day purchase
In a shopping bag,
And a Peter Rabbit chocolate
In my raincoat pocket
For later.

Her Muse Takes Her Shopping

It begins with a nudge,
An irresistible urge to grab her pocketbook and coat.
It is time again to hunt and gather treasures.
For her still-life vision,
Framed in gold and blue,
Her muse takes her shopping at flea markets.

For ceramics and glassware,
That exhibit exquisite contrasts and contours,
Perhaps this delftware crock?
Or this porcelain bud vase?
She buys them both without hesitation.
Her muse takes her shopping at garage sales.

Visual rapture unveils itself to her
In a mint green china cup missing the saucer.
Never mind the gold worn around the rim.
That can be restored with a mere brush stroke,
As spirit quickens on canvass.
Her muse takes her shopping at antique malls.

She sees this vase filled
     with yellow chrysanthemums.
There is no crack.

She sees that brass urn brimming
     with red poppies.
There is no mar.

She sees a crystal biscuit jar overflowing
	with purple cosmos.
There is no discoloration.

She sees a figurine resting gently
	against violets.
There is no stain.

Inspiration becomes tangible.
It is perfection,
Hanging majestically on a wall over a divan.

The colored chalk is the instrument
That infuses life.
Pregnant with joy,
Her muse stands back and smiles
Her approval.

Kneeling Nun

Dusky robes drape the ground
In clandestine folds.
Head bowed,
Hands clasped,
She whispers pious platitudes
Of self-admonishment
To a towering rock altar.
"Forgive me father, for I have sinned."
An image
Of virtue,
Veneration,
And reverence
Against the shadows of the hillside.
The taste of communion wine
Still lingers, fresh on her tongue.
Coral rosary beads clutched,
Their essence ferried on the wind.
Immersed in catharsis
She does not see
That God answers her prayer
With a resplendent sky of flames.

(This poem is about a landmark rock formation
located near Silver City, New Mexico.)

VISITORS TO PEARL HARBOR

Japanese tourists here
Stand on the platform,
Peer over the bow,
Snap hundreds of photos,
And gaze upon
The 1,177 names, etched
Into the white marble wall
Of the U.S.S. Arizona Memorial.
Scanning the list of
The men still entombed
In the sunken hull....is it
Pride, or guilt,
Indifference, or sadness,
Victory, or remorse?
Curiosity challenges one
To know how it feels to be
Japanese tourists here.

Temptress Muse

These four office walls
Stifle,
Oppress,
And confuse
My muse today.

"Look out the window," she beckons.
What better than to step outside
Inhale fresh air.
Unbutton the suit jacket,
Kick off those heels,
And exchange stuffy attire
For dungarees, a t-shirt,
And a light blue ribbon
For my hair.

I'll skip out the door
Stand in gleaming sunbeams,
Without sunscreen or a hat.
People may stare
At this recklessness,
So uncharacteristic.

My muse and I will pay no nevermind.
We will slide down the banister
And step on sidewalk cracks.
There's no one to harm now.
We will walk along the river
Eyes closed.

We will hum familiar tunes
And bite into crisp, golden apples
Talking with our mouths full.
We will sip champagne with bubbles
From expensive crystal glasses
Until we become giddy.
Unbridled thoughts
Explode off the page.

This temptress muse
Opens the door to a dual reality
Where children are clothed,
And fed,
And put to bed
With a pinch of glitter,
And the best of intentions.

Running Late on a Rainy Day

Silver teaspoon
Swirls the cream into the
Acidic brown brew
That provides the liquid jolt
Needed to revive the senses.
Cold pizza crosses the lips
To provide nutritional sustenance
To raise the blood sugar
Before the journey.
The stomach greets breakfast
With a sad longing for
Yesterday's glazed Krispy Kreme.
My watch chides me,
As I bolt out the door,
Briefcase in hand,
Purse slung over my shoulder,
Carrying a sweater,
My daytimer,
And a collapsible umbrella,
In case menacing dark clouds
Bring rain.

She Indulges in Red and Escargot

Succulent, scarlet strawberries…
Ripe, robust raspberries…
Comely, cabernet-colored cherries…
These attract the attention
And whet the appetite
Of the hungry turtle.
She selectively devours the red
With a satisfied snap.
In a cascade of sunshine,
Juices dribble down her chin,
Which she dabs away
With her free appendages.
Like debris
She saunters through…
Green grapes,
Fresh spinach leaves,
Radishes,
Cantaloupe wedges,
Golden apples and apricots still on the plate.
She moves onward down the lawn,
Carrying her picnic table
On her back,
Continuing the search
For savory snails.

WAITING AT THE CINCINNATI AIRPORT

The lady with the pea green pumps…sits

With crossed arms,
Crossed legs,
Pursed lips.

She checks her watch,
Clutches her handbag,
Drums her fingers,
Follows other passengers
Up and down the aisle
With her eyes.

Focused, tense, annoyed.

The lady with the blond French twist…fondles

Her diamond earrings,
Her gold necklace,
And her manicured nails.

She massages the strap
On her designer carry-on with
A prominently displayed label.
She applies red lipstick,
Swings her leg,
Adjusts her skirt.

Impatient, bored, self-absorbed.

The man in the pin-striped business suit...plants

Both feet on the floor,
Repositions his glasses,
And yawns broadly.

He flips through pages
Of a self-help novel,
Contemplating ways to get ahead.
His hands rest on the
Economical travel bag
Packed only for an overnight stay.

Passing time, relaxed, self-assured.

The boy with the blond buzz-cut...wipes

His hand on his shorts,
Spills on his shirt,
Takes another large bite.

Munching his donut and
Slurping his coffee,
He rests his arm on his
Bulging backpack,
"Catch the Wave"
It says on his hot pink t-shirt.

Testosterone-revved, snacking, ready to board.

The lady in spectacles sits, very still....observing.

Wearing tennis shoes,
A white, cotton sweater,
An elbow rests on her big, black purse.

She writes notes,
And makes assumptions...from
Body language, unconsciously
Displayed by fellow travelers...
Peering into their baggage
From a distance,
Pondering their thoughts.

Killing time, musing, amused.

Transcending the Walls of Zion

Each step along the footpath
Brings focus to the moment.
Windswept ridges along the canyon rim
Tower above.
Ragged walls of ochre and red
Emanate vibrant hues
Of magnificence.
Cascade of spring water
Tumbles down the slope
Chattering as it greets and mingles
With the rush of rapids below.
Emerald pools brim with
Abundant runoff.
The Great White Throne
And Angels Landing
Peer down in sentinel silence.
Be still…and listen.
Inner ears hear.
Inner eyes see.
Dormant senses awaken.
The soul opens…and inhales,
As it has never breathed life before.
Drink in the swell
Of indescribable ecstasy
That transcends
The walls of Zion.

Spell of the Hoodoos

"Legend People"
Turned to stone by Coyote
Say the Paiutes.
Enchanted coral and crimson hoodoos
Cast a bewitching spell
On those who gaze
Upon the canyon formations.
Pillars of fire,
Spires, columns, and arches
Eroded by time.
Still.
Silent.
Stoic red-painted faces
Reflect vermilion,
Jasper, carnelian
Scarlet and cerise
In a timeless wash of colored
Sandstone.
Kaleidoscopic majesty
Defies Kodachrome.
Vigil sovereigns
Reflect eternal sunset
As priceless, ruddy
Jewels.

Planting the Anguish in Teal

I unswaddle
The tightly wrapped
Bulb of anguish I carry
In a folded, teal napkin,
And plant it gently
In hallowed ground.
Ashes of happy memories,
Passion, pride, and pain
Are sprinkled on top.
A spade full of sand fills in quickly
The space surrounding
The still partially exposed,
Swollen package.

At last, I pat the warm sand
With the hand
That shook yours
To say good-bye.
With one hesitant step…
And then another…
I walk away,
My heart a polished stone.

I try not to think
About the shaft of green
That may break through
The amber sand in June.

Echoes of Life at Leaf Water

Golden cottonwood leaves
Along the riverbanks
Shimmer like fluttering coins.
A warm breeze dances up the hillside
Agitating taupe sand granules
And wolfberry bushes on the ridge,
At the ruins
Of Leaf Water Pueblo.

Biscuitware pottery shards,
A few smooth stone metates,
And granules of pollen
Are among the scattered remains.

A thriving community
Once nested on this bluff
Overlooking the Chama River
As it meandered through the valley.

Sedentary farmers gathered squash,
Corn, beans, and cotton
From grid-shaped garden plots.

Villagers thrived in the plaza
Children's laughter reverberated off pueblo walls
Mothers ground corn
While babies dreamed
Under a soft, blue blanket of sky.

Mountains in the distance
Stand like headstones
Bearing witness
To those who once lived here…
And moved on.

Still stirred
By a warm autumn wind
Are the echoes of life
At Leaf Water.

BUILDING A SAND CASTLE

Under plentiful sunshine
Mounds of white sand
Pressed into a bucket
Were tipped over
And emptied
To become towers…
And turrets…
And the foundation
Of a fortress.

With wet hair,
Sunburned faces,
And sand granules between our toes,
We felt safe.
We were close.

My brother and I
Shared these moments,
Tirelessly working
To create a masterpiece
While the rhythmic ocean roars
Were at bay
In the background.

We pressed our hands together
One over the other
To make one, large bucket
For the lighthouse tower...
Needed to protect our creation from
Future gale storms...
Which eventually came
And reclaimed the sand
Eroding away our creation
At high tide.

He is gone now.

I have only these memories
Of building our sand castle.

In my mind,
The rhythmic ocean roars
Are still at bay

Freeway Frenzy

Bobbing and darting through traffic
His intentions are clear.
Must be first in line on the freeway,
Cell phone stuck to his ear.

Faster now! Hits the brakes!
Cuts someone off. Can't bear to wait.
Bubbling irritation now seethes,
At his vanity L.A. license plate.

Subtle maneuver and acceleration
Now draw closed the space.
Little red sports car driver…
Is now "red" in the face.

In his tight little box,
He has to slow down.
Lips seen to utter profanities…
And choice curse words abound.

No blinkers. No manners.
No sense of fair play.
I helped teach a California driver
The lesson of "mañana" today.

Apricot Moments

Apricot honey
Softened by mist
Velvety breath
As petal-soft kissed.

Electric moments ecstatic
Tender trembling bliss
Memories of new love
Are colored like this.

LURE OF THE SIRENS

How lucky do you feel tonight?
When you hear the melodic slot machines
Serenade with Siren songs?
The tempting chortle of bells and chimes,
The clank of an arm dropping to initiate a spin,
Or the repetitious thud of coins dropping
In a cavernous, metal mouth.
The shrill ring of a winning machine,
Two seats down, seduces.
Mechanical procurer of silver
From the pockets and purses
Of persons become zombies.

Watch the animated metal slot
Consume, swallow, and gulp
Quarters, nickels, and dollars
With insatiable appetite.
Preying on greed and weakness
With "quick-fix" promises
Of instant wealth.

Coaxing colors tease.
Spinning fruit mesmerizes.
Flashing buttons beckon.
Cheerful noises allure.
Such a clever, gilded deception
Raucous temptation lilts
Down every aisle
And smoke-filled passageway.

Hawking promises:
"Play with me!"
"Be a winner!"
"Redeem your soul and your value here!"
"Insert a coin, and take a chance!"
"How lucky do you feel tonight?"

WIND WHISPERS

White,
Whimsical
Dandelion puff
Captured
By lilting breezes.
Feather-soft seeds scatter
Aloft,
Airborne,
Animated,
Whispering.

This is When I Think of You

This is when
I think of you...
When twilight skies
Wash lapis blue.

When arid wind
Swirls warm and brisk,
And wafts the scent
Of tamarisk.

About the Author

Karin Stangl is a poet from Albuquerque, New Mexico. She is a member of New Mexico Poetry Alliance, New Mexico Poetry Society, PoetSeven and Fresh Ink writing groups.

Her award-winning poetry has been published in *Muse with Blue Apples, Willow Street Magazine, Turtle Music Anthology, Crosswinds Magazine, The Southwest Poet, Compass Points,* and *Along the Rio Grande: Poetry from New Mexico,* among other publications. She has bachelor's and master's degrees from the University of New Mexico. She is currently a public relations consultant in Albuquerque.

Acknowledgements

"Echoes of Life at Leaf Water" was published in the anthology *Adobe Walls #5* in 2013.

"Ode to Fruitcake" and "She Indulges in Red and Escargot" were published in the anthology *Turtle Music* in 2011.

"Savor the Wine and Chocolate" was published in the *Beaujolais et Poesie* by L'Alliance Francaise d'Albuquerque in 2011.

"This Is When I Think of You" won an Honorable Mention in the To a Wild Rose Poetry Contest in 2010.

"Rain Stick" was published in *Compass Points* in 2002, *Willow Street Magazine* in 2000, and in *Crosswinds Weekly* in 1999.

"Age Is a Matter of Mind" was published in *Compass Points* in 2002 and received an Honorable Mention from the New Mexico State Poetry Society Contest in 2001.

"Carousel" received a Second Place Award from the New Mexico State Poetry Society Contest in 2001.

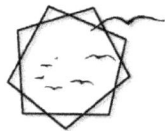

www.ingramcontent.com/pod-product-compliance
Lightning Source LLC
Chambersburg PA
CBHW030155070426
42447CB00032B/1207